My DESTINY HELPER

Practical guide to encountering your destiny helper

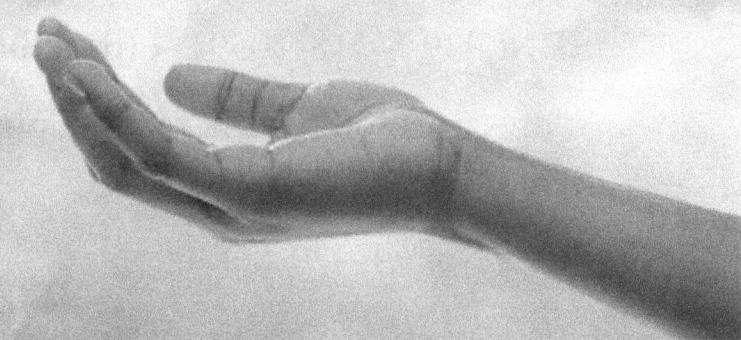

ABIMBOLA OMENE

COPYRIGHT

Copyright © 2022 by Abimbola Omene.

All rights reserved. No part of this publication may be reproduced, distributed, or transmitted in any form or by any means, including photocopying, recording, or other electronic or mechanical methods, without the prior written permission of the publisher, except in the case of brief quotations embodied in critical reviews and certain other noncommercial uses permitted by copyright law. For permission requests, write to the publisher:

First Printing: November, 2022.

ISBN: 979-8-218-10591-4 (paperback).

Address: 13300 Morris road, Alpharetta GA 30004, US.

Phone No: +1-470-668-0255

Email Address: bimsybooks@gmail.com

DEDICATION

This book is dedicated to almighty God, my father. Thank you for saving me over and over again.

MY DESTINY HELPER

TABLE OF CONTENTS

COPYRIGHT 2

DEDICATION 3

PREFACE 6

CHAPTER 1 7

WHO IS A DESTINY HELPER 7

CHAPTER 2 19

MEETING MY DESTINY HELPER 19

CHAPTER 3 35

THE ENCOUNTER 35

CHAPTER 4 39

THE LESSONS 39

SALVATION 47

FEEDBACK 49

ABOUT THE AUTHOR 50

PREFACE

We all need people. The saying is true – No man is an island. When we pray, answers mostly come through humans. In our walk through life we need to be mindful of how we treat or relate with people.

"Don't forget to show hospitality to strangers. For some who have done this have entertained angels without realizing it!"

- Hebrews 13:2. NLT

CHAPTER 1

WHO IS A DESTINY HELPER

"God alone raises men, but He does it through other men".

The concept of destiny helper is one that has gathered dust across several groups and spheres. It is typically the realization that man is constrained and, to be honest, crippled to support himself through the difficult voyages of life. Without a doubt, God created humanity with a supernatural strength that astounded even celestial creatures, who asked, "What is man that you are so watchful of?" However, in order for man to exist and fulfill purpose in this earthly realm, he needs destiny helpers. No man that God created is independent of the assistance of other men. Whether you are wealthy, poor, or well-liked, you need assistance in order to advance in life and keep up a nice existence.

Why You Need Help

"I know the thoughts that I think toward you, saith the Lord, thoughts of peace, and not of evil, to give you an expected end."

- Jerimiah 29.11 KJV

What is our destination? In order to learn more, man reads the news, listens to the radio, and watches television to learn about current events. What's going on in the world, what's happening to man, what does man do to man, and where is the world going? Man will eventually come upon the purpose question in the midst of all this confusion. According to an author, everybody is born pregnant. This proves that we all have a problem-solving mechanism within of us. We all have a purpose for being here on earth; for you, it might be to raise a generation of Christians; for others, it might be something as noble as raising your children.

In the words of Swami Chidananda, "You are not who you are right now. This is a fallen state. The opportunity to be born as a being with feelings, thoughts, and reasoning allows you to consider your own life and rediscover your previous divine existence. You are in a state of perfect purity. The state of man is that of a paradise lost; his ultimate fate is that of a paradise recovered."

In order to help us fulfill God's plan for our lives, He provides us with destiny helpers. The paradox is that many people who help us fulfill God's plans for us barely even realize they are doing so. When we are in a desperate situation, different kinds of destiny helpers are assigned to cross our paths. The Holy Spirit, angelic and human assistants of destiny are all at your disposal. God's plan included using Pharaoh's daughter to save the infant Moses (Exodus 2:1-10). Ruth was Naomi's partner in destiny.

I must first make it obvious to you that unless God acts on behalf of another individual, no one can help that man. This explains why some individuals come so close to getting help but never do. The best potential illustration of this is the man's life at the pool in Bethesda. It had to take God himself to come to his aide.

Simply recording the development of a bud from its initial appearance until it blooms into a full flower can help us understand destiny. Something that is hidden and seems so insignificant actually contains greatness, if only you will look with different eyes, you might be able to see the enormous dynamism, the creation of the softness of the petals, the exquisite colors and the magnetism.

As the bud develops, the inner beauty gradually becomes more apparent. This is how we humans are. A number of people see themselves insignificant, but just like a bud that becomes a flower—which is destiny, humans have the innate ability to reach their full potential.

So, just as a flower needs assistance planting, weeding, and watering in order to grow naturally, men also need assistance from other men in order to fulfill their potential. This is what destiny helper actually means. Even if working hard is important, if it were the only thing influencing your development, it would be miserable. No one has ever prospered by hard work alone. Work by itself won't raise a man's status. The Bible states that,

"Time and chance happeneth to them all," noting that **"the race is not to the swift, nor the battle to the strong, neither yet bread to the wise, nor yet riches to men of understanding, nor yet favor to men of skill."**

- *Ecclesiastes 9:11 KJV*

Apostle Joshua Selman once said in one of his sermons: "it matters not who hates you in the kingdom but who likes you." This is very profound. Many7 people lose out on opportunities to advance because they have preconceived notions about what a destiny helper ought to resemble.

An opponent of advancement could on occasion be advantageous. What makes me say that? After receiving a false accusation from Potiphar's wife, Joseph was put in prison. The fact that Joseph was in prison was an extremely awful situation. Nonetheless, God was kind to Joseph while he was imprisoned. He was successful there too. It is important to know that help is always time bound. Even if you locate the person who is meant to be your aid right immediately, it can take months or even years before you receive any genuine assistance. Also, the help might not be required immediately, but it is wise to create the link.

Your ability to acknowledge, embrace, value, enjoy, seek out, and exult in the people God has put in your path is the key to achieving your destiny.

The meeting of our chosen helpers has been divinely prepared. God makes use of assistants to further His goal or plan for our lives. God will send us defenders who will defend us and create doors for us to advance. In other instances, God sends helpers to a divine location to aid us or raises them suddenly in the middle of our situation. We need to ask God to help us remember our allies. Location is essential for both the fulfillment of divine purpose and for others to find us.

We have all heard incredible stories of how angelic interventions have helped God's children through difficult times. Even now, angels are still sent on missions to deliver and save God's children. Angels of destiny rescued Daniel after his adversaries forced him into the lion's den. After Daniel had fasted for twenty-one days, an angel of destiny sent an emissary to deliver a message. The Prince of Persia first opposed the angel until another angel, Michael, was sent to help the angel.

God helped Naaman in 2 Kings 5:3 through a maid. God can use anyone to help you. He had leprosy despite being a wealthy general, demonstrating that not everything that money can buy is worthwhile. Despite his wealth, Naaman thought leprosy was shameful. His destiny helper was the small maid in 2 Kings 5:3; she recommended him to take a wash in the pool, which he did, and he recovered. Naaman was escorted to a prophet in Israel, where he was shocked to see that he was instructed to bathe in a deplorable pool rather than bring a servant. The man declined out of pride.

"Manna only falls from heaven when you have someone at the top showering it down on you". Michael Bassey Johnson.

This brings to mind my personal experience of an angelic encounter. A couple of years ago I had to undergo an emergency surgery due to a sudden condition, and as always God intervened to save me. The day after my surgery, an angel visited me in my hospital room. The angel in the appearance of a woman came in and sat by my bed. What was very striking was she had a completely dark and beautiful complexion with a shinning light on her forehead and a big smile as she spoke. She said she had come to encourage me and let me know that God said what I had been praying for had been granted. Several minutes later, I stepped outside my room to ask about the woman who had just disappeared, but they claimed that nobody had entered through the door.

CHAPTER 2

MEETING MY DESTINY HELPER

I went to church on a regular Sunday, expecting to have a spiritual encounter with God as is usually the case, but I had no idea that day would also bring me face to face with a man. It was sometime in October, my home church occasionally invites ministers of God to serve in the church, and this day was one of those occasions. I usually greet visiting guest clergy at church after the service and give them cash gifts in addition to my respect. I've grown to identify with this nature. However, that day was different since I was in a bad financial situation and had only enough cash on me to get me through the week. Despite this constraint, I grabbed for my wallet and gave my last. I wasn't trying to be brave; I wasn't sure where I would get the money for the following day, but I felt compelled to just give him everything. I was guided by the Holy Spirit and my intuition—I am a giver.

"A man's gift maketh room for him, and bringeth him before great men."

- Proverbs 18:16 KJV

I used to think this scripture was referring to a man's talent alone until my encounter with this minister of God.

Two weeks later, I hardly recall how I managed to get by. During the two weeks that preceded my first interaction with him, the man of God came to the church, but this time it wasn't for another ministration. I found myself in the company of this man and he wanted to thank me for the cash gift, and also give a word of prayer. As he began to pray, he gave me a word of prophecy, telling me that I would meet my destiny helper in 21 days (3 weeks). Since it wasn't the first time I'd gotten a prophecy, I wasn't as surprised as I might have been. I responded by saying, "Amen," as he prayed, and then calculated that the 21 days would be around that year's Thanksgiving. Could this be real, and why on Thanksgiving? Everything appeared to be a puzzle that I was anxious to solve.

"But, beloved, be not ignorant of this one thing, that one day is with the Lord as a thousand years, and a thousand years as one day."

- 2 Peter 3:8. KJV

I eagerly anticipated finding comfort in the aforementioned text, but instead, three years passed instead of 3 weeks. Of course at this point, a lot of questions started to arise: was this prophecy accurate? Had God forgotten what he had said? Does this delay mean that I am being denied? Those thoughts flooded in, and it's natural for them too. Even the bible says,

"Hope deferred makes the heart sick, but a dream fulfilled is a tree of life."

- *Proverbs 13:12. NLT*

Can you recall a time when you received a prophecy and were quite certain that it was from God, but it did not turn out the way you had hoped? Many other things could have contributed to its occurrence. However, there is only one absolute truth.

"God is not a man, that he should lie; neither the son of man, that he should repent: hath he said, and shall he not do it? Or hath he spoken, and shall he not make it good?"

- *Numbers 23:19 KJV*

If God is the one who spoke, there may seem to be a delay, but there is never a denial. God doesn't always cause delays;

occasionally, you have to fulfill a prerequisite in order to fulfill a certain prophecy. However, many people who hear the prophecy choose to sit back and do nothing, this is what could cause a delay.

Prophecies are time-bound and can only be fulfilled up until a specific date. The recipient of a prophetic word is urged to engage the word in prayer regardless of the type of prophecy they have received.

"Then Elijah said to Ahab, "Go get something to eat and drink, for I hear a mighty rainstorm coming!

So Ahab went to eat and drink. But Elijah climbed to the top of Mount Carmel and bowed low to the ground and prayed with his face between his knees."

- 1 Kings 18: 41-42. NLT

Elijah had a prophetic word, and his immediate action was to go in for prayers. This is the right posture you take. After prayers then you must come to the place of rest and waiting on the lord. Never give up. God always knows the right time.

Years passed and it was 2015. I belonged to a prayer group where we share the word, pray and edify one another in the lord. That year, there was a teaching series going on, and it was on the importance of showing kindness to people as you never know who God has sent to you. Being a good Samaritan, just like the proverbial man in the bible who helped the helpless man on the street who was half dead, is a lesson we have all heard and been taught since we were young children. Our parents would say it, and our local children's pastor would follow suit. As usual, I took in that teaching and jotted down some key points in my notes.

I got dressed and drove out to run a few errands one afternoon in May. I suddenly stopped and parked as I was leaving the area. I didn't know why I had parked, as if I were expecting to pick up or attend to someone. I thought it was a little mystical because this had never occurred to me before. As I was still in my car and lost in thought, a young girl approached me and said that her auntie makes hair and that I should go see her. She could hardly speak English, but there was something odd about the way she just showed up at my door to introduce herself and promote her auntie's business.

Instead of acting out of fear or treating her like an unwanted solicitor as would have been a normal reaction, I requested for the name, phone number, or address of her auntie. She didn't have any, but after saying that she said she could go ask and she ran off. What am I doing I asked myself, an homeless young girl? This made me even more worried.

"The steps of a good man are ordered by the LORD: and he delighteth in his way."

- Psalm 37. 23. KJV

After sometime, as I sat in my car trying to remember where I was going and what I was going to do, the child ran back to me with a piece of paper with a phone number, and the name of the auntie. I was simply waiting for someone to yell cut! Since it appeared as though I was mysteriously pulled into the center of a movie set. The odd thing was that I had forgotten why I came out by this time. So I made the decision to call the number and speak with this mysterious auntie. Following initial introductions and questions, we both decided to meet up at a specific time the same day.

In helping others, we receive help - we help ourselves.

"A man that hath friends must shew himself friendly."

- Proverbs 18: 24.KJV

The time has come to meet the mysterious woman who answered the phone. The secret started to become clear when I approached her and she introduced herself. She mentioned that she had recently relocated here from another country, and I went ahead to give her a lot of helpful information and advice to make their transition go well. I also let her know she may call me at any time if she needed anything. It seemed like we had known each other for a very long time as we spoke for about two hours.

I went out of my way during the following weeks to make the family feel at home.

They didn't have a car, so I frequently ran errands to the grocery store, often paying for the groceries even though I was barely getting by on my own. I assisted with registration, immunization records, and other school-related tasks for the kids. As if that wasn't enough, I referred her to a friend of mine who also took the initiative to drive them to church each Sunday and assist in any other manner they could. I was simply pleased to be able to assist a family in need, as was my friend.

"…The zeal of the LORD of hosts will perform this."

- Isaiah 9. 7. KJV

After a few weeks, I realized that this woman was taking undue advantage of both my friend and me. She started to tell unreliable tales and would fabricate information to gain benefits. This should have been a cue for me to back off, but instead, I felt compelled to continue assisting them.

Also, my husband had just returned from a trip and I introduced him to her family. Her husband got along well with mine and It wasn't long when he requested financial assistance from my husband. When my husband told me about it, I simply advised him to offer help however he could.

This is a crucial lesson. God sometimes sends us to help imperfect people; in fact, the true test of love is when He places you right in the middle of your enemy and asks you to assist them. How would you respond?

"The LORD said to Hosea, 'Go, take unto thee a wife of whoredoms and have children of whoredoms."

- Hosea 1:2. KJV

Hosea obeyed, marrying a woman named Gomer, who was unfaithful to him.

For what purpose did God command Hosea to wed a prostitute? Do not forget that Hosea was a prophet. But God intended to use the tale of Hosea and Gomer as a metaphor for His love for His children. Hosea's steadfast love for Gomer serves as an example of God's steadfast love for Israel's rebellion.

God is always up to something when he puts us in difficult situations.

Some of my family members had actually realized that she was abusing her power, taking unfair advantage of my goodwill to her. But that didn't change my mind much; I still forged ahead in helping her.

This woman revealed to me one day that she fasts and prays in the late afternoon. I was initially taken aback. Not because of a sense of superiority, but only to meet the requirements in 1 John 4:1,

"Beloved, do not believe every spirit, but test the spirits to see whether they are from God...."

Because I didn't want to become involved with something that was not of God, I was becoming a little weary of this. I observed her progressively acquiring this remarkable gift as she continued to fast, pray, and wait on the Lord. I was still being very helpful during all of this.

We tried to schedule our prayers together during this time, but for some reason it never worked out.

CHAPTER 3

THE ENCOUNTER

I went shopping at the start of the Thanksgiving holiday that year and bought a feast for her and her family, as she was in a very challenging situation, so I made an effort to cheer her up and help her experience the spirit of Thanksgiving. She was so appreciative that she requested that we pray together. So we began to pray every day for our families and other concerns.

Again, the bible verse, Proverbs 18:16 KJV, "A man's gift maketh room for him," came to mind once more as it had done in October of that year.

The woman was then revealed to me by God as my destiny helper, and He began to talk to me about it. However, until one of our prayer meetings, it wasn't entirely clear. I've been following this woman's prayer and fasting journey for a few weeks, and I've seen her supernaturally develop in her spiritual gift. In my brief time as a Christian, I had never witnessed such a strange gift. I had no idea I would be a beneficiary of this gift.

During one of her prayer sessions, I joined her to pray and the strangest things began to occur. She interceded on my behalf concerning a long fought battle I had almost gave up on and through the help of the Holy Spirit, she was able to win a major spiritual battle on my behalf.

Immediately, my mind flashed back to the prophetic word that was given to me by the guest minister, and then I realized that it was exactly 3 years from the 21 days (3 weeks) of the prophesy.

I think what kept me going for the three years was my understanding of the prophetic message. I occasionally ponder if I would have been patient or encouraged if the word had said three years. The oddest part was that the woman had also told me at the time that I was her destiny helper. My understanding of it was foggy but it seemed to be like a puzzle that was slowly fitting together.

MY DESTINY HELPER

CHAPTER 4

THE LESSONS

Looking back, four months before the whole episode, my prayer group topic was on how to treat your destiny helper. There is always a preparation period.

"Let your character [your moral essence, your inner nature] be free from the love of money [shun greed—be financially ethical], being content with what you have; for He has said, "I WILL NEVER" [under any circumstances] DESERT YOU [nor give you up nor leave you without support, nor will I in any degree leave you helpless], NOR WILL I

FORSAKE OR LET YOU DOWN OR RELAX MY HOLD ON YOU [assuredly not]!"

- Hebrews 13: 5 AMP

While I was awaiting God, he prepared me. The connection would have been lost if I had not been kind and helpful to the woman when I first met her. I could have disregarded the little girl who first approached me as a solicitor. The adversary tried several times to keep us apart by showing me her ugly side, but God gave me the wisdom and grace to forbear.

There is a time and a season for everything.

"And of the children of Issachar, which were men that had understanding of the times, to know what Israel ought to do; the heads of them were two hundred; and all their brethren were at their commandment."

- 1 chronicles 12: 32 KJV

We need to be as attentive of our times and seasons as the sons of Issachar were. The mission was completed and the crucial battle was won.

In encountering your destiny helper, there is a tendency to glorify him rather than glorify who sent him. Yes, they are meant to help you in a particular circumstance, but they are only God's servants, not the Lord. Make sure you worship the creator, the omnipotent

God, the beginning and the end rather than the creation. Even from the outset, he is aware of the outcome. Give him praise!

Most of the time, your destiny helper won't arrive wearing a sign on their forehead. She had not even developed her gift when we first met. Based on how the young girl approached me, I might have easily dismissed her when she first approached me, thinking she was soliciting. It is very important to never belittle anyone.

"Don't forget to show hospitality to strangers, for some who have done this have entertained angels without realizing it!"

- Hebrews 13.2 NLT

Our understanding of the prophecy was 3 weeks. But in reality it was 3 years.

"The Lord is not slack concerning *His* promise, as some count slackness, but is longsuffering toward us, not willing that any should perish but that all should come to repentance."

- 2 Peter 3:9 NKJV

While you are waiting, you need to keep busy in preparation, serving and doing the father's business.

"For the Father loves the Son and shows him everything he is doing. In fact, the Father will show him how to do even greater works than healing this man. Then you will truly be astonished."

- John 5:20 NLT

That is another important thing to remember. It is wise to let go of someone or something gracefully after their time in your life is through.

"But I say unto you, Love your enemies, bless them that curse you, do good to them that hate you, and pray for them which despitefully use you, and persecute you…"

- Matthew 5:44 KJV

Prayerfully, God caused the separation. The woman and her family moved out of the neighborhood for reasons best known to them.

The first and primary aider of destiny is the All-Powerful God. The original promoter, he lifts your head, positions individuals to help you, and he has the authority to demote one person in order to promote another. He stands up for the defenseless. You ask your uncle or your boss for help, but keep in mind that no one can help you unless your alignment with God is strong.

Being an adversary of God will prevent you from fulfilling your potential.

Looking unto Jesus the author and finisher of our faith; who for the joy that was set before him endured the cross, despising the shame, and is set down at the right hand of the throne of God.

- Hebrews 12:2

I believe by the time you're done reading this book, you'd be bursting out with testimonies of destiny helpers assisting you in your life. Amen.

SALVATION

You can only be helped by God, and he only employs men to do so, just as it was written in this book. Therefore, it is necessary for man to discover God in order to fulfill his or her life's purpose. If you feel a nudge to rededicate or give your life to Christ after reading this book, please say this prayer:

Lord Jesus, I confess my sins and surrender my life to you. Please come into my heart as my Lord and Savior. Take complete control of my life and help me to walk in your footsteps daily by the power of the Holy Spirit. I acknowledge that you died for my sins. Thank you Lord for saving me and for answering my prayer. Amen.

If you said that prayer, please find a bible believing church to attend or get in touch with me.

FEEDBACK

For feedback about this book and any question(s) relating to the content of this book and other interests, please write to me:

Email: bimsybooks@gmail.com

Phone: +1-470-668-0255

To order copies of my book (e-book and paperback) visit Amazon Kindle, Apple Books and other book merchants.

ABOUT THE AUTHOR

Abimbola Omene is a passionate writer who doubles as an exceptional leader and selfless giver. She takes great joy in imparting God's truth and wisdom, in teaching and encouraging individuals from various social classes and age groups. She is married to a wonderful man of God and has lovely children.